Us Ordinary Folk

Previous Books:

Exposed to Winds
[Selected poems]

Construction Delay Claims
[Performance measurements]

Anecdotes of Would-be Experts
[Business experiences]

Thoughts in a Maze
[Various mysteries]

Trials and Errors
[Life experiences]

Characters

Oddities

Connections

Conclusions Volumes I & II

My Best Dog Days

Investment Fundamentals

Our Support Systems

About My Books

Human Traits & Follies

Honesty's Travesty

Critical Reflections

Us Ordinary Folk

by

Arthur O.R. Thormann

Specfab Industries Ltd.

Edmonton, Alberta

2018

Thormann, Arthur O. R. (Arthur Otto Rudolf), 1934-, author
    Us Ordinary Folk

ISBN 978-0-9916849-7-7

Publisher: Specfab Industries Ltd.
                    13559 - 123A Avenue
                    Edmonton, Alberta, Canada
                    T5L 2Z1
                    Telephone: 780-454-6396

Publication assistance by

PAGEMASTER
PUBLISHING
PageMaster.ca

Cover Designs: Front: Figure of a relaxing hobo
                    Back: Text by author; sunflower seeds depict us
                    ordinary folk, and the petals depict our celebrities

We can't help everyone, but everyone can help someone.
Ronald Reagan

The purpose of human life is to serve, and to show compassion and the will to help others.
Albert Schweitzer

I believe in Spinoza's God who reveals himself in the ordinary harmony of what exists, not a God who concerns himself with the fates and actions of human beings.
Albert Einstein

I dedicate this book to all us ordinary folk in life!

Preface

Ordinary folk often fail to understand what's happening on the world scene and even closer to home. We ordinary folk depend for our understanding on what bigwigs decide we should know and on the media, even though the media may put their own spin on the so-called news. This leads to speculations and misunderstandings. The reluctance of bigwigs to be open is often understandable, and the dramatization of the news by the media is also understandable, but it forces us to make up our own minds to know what is happening and what is true.

Regardless how twisted the media may present us with the news, I for one value our media. The reason is that I experienced a state-controlled media in my early life, and with that sort of media we are often purposely misled. Our free-world media may put their own spin on the news, but they seldom purposely tell us lies!

We are well aware of what famous people have done to become famous, and my aim for this book was to interview some of us ordinary folk to find out what they do and believe, and how they fulfill their purpose in life.

Also, I wanted to explore a bit about the purpose of human life. Let me start by telling you my belief: I think the purpose of human life is to advance the human race. Whether you have attained fame or are just one of us ordinary folk, the purpose is the same, although we may not realize it.

Let me illustrate this point by a brick building: The bricks, akin to famous people, are very visible, but the mortars, akin to us ordinary folk, are very necessary to hold the bricks together. Both, the bricks and the mortars form a strong building, akin to an advanced human race.

The advancement of the human race aims at a more harmonious life, as our fellow on the front cover of this book has already attained.

The fellow on the front cover is obviously oblivious to what's happening around him, especially world events, not because he doesn't care about them, but because he gave up speculating on them. So, since he is one of us ordinary folk, perhaps we can try to inspire him to take notice with a few of our own speculations.

All of the chapters aim to address aspects of human life that are everyday concerns of us ordinary folk, and the appendix aims to inspire millionaires to do their part to advance the human race.

Arthur O.R. Thormann
May 2018

Contents

Introduction: A Born Critic

If anyone can be born anything, I think I am a born critic. Even during my babyhood I was a critic of my parents. I still remember my parents discussing what to do with me while they were out going to see a movie – no TVs in those days, and they didn't have a baby sitter. They finally decided I would probably fall asleep, and, in any case, I could not be able to climb out of my crib. Two hours later, when they came back, I was standing up in the crib with my hands on the top rail and cried out "ha," criticizing them for leaving me alone. That was my earliest experience as a critic. A few years later, when my parents sent me to Sunday school, I criticized the Bible stories the Sunday school teacher told us. I thought the Brothers Grimm's stories made more sense.

Then, as a teenager, I criticized my math teacher for failing to give me an algebraic equation for a straight line sloping down to the X line and then up again away from it. The math teacher challenged me to work out an equation for it, and I came up with an answer by multiplying the equation of the line sloping down by the equation of the line sloping up. The teacher was amazed after testing my answer on the blackboard, but did not seem happy. The teacher had the typical adult attitude despising smart aleck teenagers. I was only happy that I had stumbled upon the answer to a difficult problem. Upstaging the teacher had not even entered my mind.

Do I dare criticize God? The answer is no if we mean by God the Supreme Existence in the Universe, namely our Universal Laws. But I do not hesitate to criticize the creators of the Biblical God, who, to me, is nothing more than an emotional Being who was given special powers by his creators – powers which are nevertheless questionable. To be sure, I'm not an atheist, but I do not believe in an emotional God, as created by the writers of the Bible. However, I firmly believe in the Supreme Existence that governs our Universe. I believe a simultaneous belief in the Supreme Existence and the Biblical God is a good example of doublethink, since only one concept can be supreme.

I have always steered clear of groups that would box in my thinking and rob me of my independence. I have never joined a church or a religious group, nor have I ever joined a political party, or groups like the Free Masons, Odd Fellows, and Technocrats. Thus, I remained free to criticize them all. Of course I'm a born German, but that never stopped me from

2

criticizing the Germans if I felt justified to do so. On November 22, 1957, I became a Canadian citizen, because I felt the Canadians were the freest thinkers I had come across, and I still think that is true. Prior to becoming a Canadian citizen, I had also spent some time with the Americans in the U.S.A., but I concluded the Canadians were freer thinkers.

Another objection I've had to joining groups is groupthink. Groupthink is a pattern of thoughts characterized by self-deception, forced manufacture of consent, and conformity to group values and ethics. That's the definition; in other words, one has to be like the group to be liked by the group. Even though I have been part of a group of trustees for many years, the group always encouraged individual-think, and groupthink never became a problem, although the group also encouraged a consensus on decisions, but a consensus based on individual-think and not groupthink. To accomplish this, the group discussed ideas until objections were resolved to everyone's satisfaction. In fact, in this group the criterion is not to be liked but to have one's ideas liked. Nevertheless, in a group of trustees unanimity is important because of potential legal consequences for mistakes.

All my life, when facing confusing issues, I quickly found some fault with them and didn't mind mentioning my criticisms to others. I now realize that this trait of mine did not make me too many loving friends. Who wants to get to the bottom of things if it often causes unhappiness? Just recently, my friend Bob Lynn ran an idea of his past me, and I criticized it. He was not happy about this and said it was unjustified. Perhaps it was, and I realized that I just acted from my natural habit of being a critic. Bob and I are both born critics, so, sometimes he will critique A while I critique B. Nevertheless, Bob is more diplomatic.

Recently, as I thought about the seventeen books I had written, I realized that all of them were full of criticism – even my poem book, Exposed to Winds. The title was taken from a poem about a stone in the middle of nowhere. Even such a simple poem describing the loneliness of a stone has criticism in it. So, why have I never written a book without criticism? The answer is simple: because I'm a born critic – I just can't help myself.

Here is a critique of myself: There are three things in my life I constantly have to watch: one is, when I get a brief brainwave, I must write it down before it disappears on me; the second is, when I'm up against stupidity, I must remind myself to be more tolerant; and the third is simply to be more diplomatic in my born criticism of others.

The Interests of Juniors

For this chapter, I decided to interview our grand-children, starting with twelve-year old Jordan. My aim for this interview was that I wanted the input of fairly young folk for this book, to give us an idea of their activities and thinking. Jordan lives in Vancouver, BC. His ancestry is German and Filipino. He's a fast learner, presently in grade seven, and a member of the groups "Destination Imagination" and "Maple Grove Math Club." To regain his strength, Jordan sleeps six to ten hours a day, depending on his level of activity.

Jordan dislikes art and finds it boring; he says he has no religion, and his philosophy is: always be humble. He believes the present school system is too easy. He loves his mother most, and his best friend is Rob, his mother's friend. His worst enemy is hesitation, and he hates an annoying girl he's met. He finds insects disgusting and spiders scare him.

Jordan's favorite pastime is eating, and his favorite food is Beef Wellington. He likes drinking Shirley Temples. His hobbies are reading and computer games, and his favorite sport is baseball, but he also likes watching basketball. His favorite movie is *Interstellar*. He finds roller coasting exciting and his teacher's stories amusing. Jordan would like to travel to Japan, and says the most memorable event in his life was a cruise to the Caribbean Islands.

Jordan says his best accomplishment was achieving the highest score in an academic test, and his worst mistake is thinking he is not being taught in school. Rude and uneducated children depress him the most, and his worst concern is North Korea starting a nuclear war. He is also concerned that men are better off than women, and that whites are better off than blacks. He has no health concerns, and does not detest any nation, but he likes Canada the most.

Jordan does not want to become a celebrity; his ambition is to run his mother's company and take it to the highest level of competence. He aspires to build his dream home one day, and he believes his life's meaning is to spend as much time with his loved ones while he is still there to see them.

Well! What do you think? Is this what you would expect to get from an interview with a twelve-year old youngster? Interesting, isn't it? And remember, he is one of us ordinary folk! How many celebrities in the world would equal his ambitions, activities, tastes, and philosophical outlook?

I also interviewed our twenty-year old grand-daughter Samantha. Samantha lives in Vancouver,

BC. Her ancestry is German and Filipino. She's bright and understands different perspectives well. She is presently in her fourth year of college, and a member of a Spanish Learning Group. To regain her strength, Samantha sleeps an average of seven hours a day.

Samantha dislikes being late, which happens too often. Being too comfortable she thinks is boring. She has no religion but believes in reincarnation, and her philosophy is looking for bliss. She loves her mother most, and she thinks her best friend, as well as her worst enemy, is herself. She hates nobody and loves her family most. Losing a loved one scares her the most, and she finds murder disgusting.

Samantha's favorite pastime is cooking healthful food for family and friends. Italian food is her favorite, and she likes drinking water. Her hobby is art, and running is her favorite sport, but she also likes watching figure skating. Her favorite movie is *The Grand Budapest Hotel*. She finds scary experiences exciting and thinks her brother Jordan is amusing. The most memorable event in her life was when her brother Jordan was born. To expand her horizon, she would like to travel to Asia.

Samantha says her best accomplishment was creating her own business in 2017, and her worst mistake was not learning enough in high school. What depresses her most is when she is mean to herself, and her worst concern is not being fulfilled and dying alone. She thinks that men are better off than women, and that whites are better off systematically than blacks. Her health concerns are being too frail.

Samantha does not dislike any nation, but she likes Canada the most. She does not want to become a celebrity, but her ambition is to inspire many people. She aspires to eventually become more like her mother, her brother Garett, her sister Megan, and her maternal grandfather. Her most cherished desire is to always be courageous, and she believes that life's meaning is for humans to love each other and to improve things.

Well, here you have a young woman's concerns, interests, and outlook on life! What do you think? Her take is somewhat different from her brother Jordan's. Does her femininity have something to do with this?

Next, I interviewed our twenty-six-year old granddaughter Megan. Megan lives in Vancouver, BC. Her ancestry is German and Filipino. She's bright and understands different perspectives well. She has a Bachelor of Commerce degree, and is a member of The Prosperous Coach Salon with Rich Litvin. She works diligently as a professional coach, and what she does best is understand different perspectives. To regain her strength, Megan sleeps an average of seven-and-a-half hours a day.

Megan dislikes doing complex mathematical calculations. She thinks TV news is boring, especially when it gets opinionated. She has no religion but believes the universe works for us. She also believes that every human being is worthy of love, and that we create our own reality. Her philosophy is to contribute to society her natural gifts. She hates nobody and loves her boyfriend Javeed most. Of her parents, she loves her mother most. Her best girlfriend is a woman named Nazlee. Losing a loved one scares her the most, and she finds black speckles that look like baby spiders disgusting. Her worst enemy is her ego.

Megan's favorite pastime is spending time with family and friends. Sushi is her favorite food, and she likes drinking mango juice. Her hobbies are dancing, card games, reading, and yin yoga, and biking is her favorite sport, but she also likes watching figure skating. Her favorite movie is *Hunger Games*. She finds helping someone improve his or her relationship exciting, and she finds cute animals and babies amusing. The most memorable event in her life was yelling at her father for putting them in danger. She likes travelling worldwide, especially to nice beaches.

Megan says her best accomplishment was graduating from university at age nineteen, and her worst mistake was when she said a terrible thing to her boyfriend Javeed that deeply hurt him. What depresses her most is when things are not working out for her, and her worst concern is not having enough money. She thinks that women and men are equal, but that women have many unrecognized influential gifts. As far as blacks and whites are concerned, she says that black people have faced many more challenges historically than white people. Her health concerns are back pain and indigestion.

Megan disapproves of North Korea, but only because of Kim Yong-un, their leader. She likes Canada the most as a nation. She does not want to become a celebrity, and her ambition is to lead a happy and prosperous life. She aspires to build a well-known coaching business, and her most cherished desire is to make a meaningful impact on the world. She believes that life's meaning is to find one's true self and to help others.

Again, here we have a young woman's concerns, interests, and outlook on life! What do you think? Her interests are somewhat different from her sister Samantha's. Does her additional education and experience have something to do with this?

I finished with our thirty-year old grandson Garett. Garett lives in Vancouver, BC. His ancestry is German and Filipino. He's bright and understands different perspectives well. He has a first-year college education, and is a member of The Whisky Tasting

Club. He works diligently as a business consultant, and what he does best is solving problems. To regain his strength, Garett sleeps eight to ten hours a day.

Garett dislikes paper work, and finds the status quo boring. His religion is Christian. He believes that anything is possible, and that there is more knowledge out there than a person can obtain in a lifetime. His philosophy is to be better today than he was yesterday. He hates computerized call centers, and loves his mother most, who is also his best friend. Accidental death scares him the most, and he finds arrogance and ignorance disgusting. His worst enemy is himself.

Garett's favorite pastime is spending time with family and friends. Japanese is his favorite food, and Scotch whisky is his favorite drink. His hobbies include reading, computer games, and personal development, and pool and basketball are his favorite sports. He also likes watching basketball. His favorite movie is *Kung Fu Panda*. He finds progression exciting, and nothing amusing. The most memorable event in his life was swimming with dolphins. He likes travelling, and his future travel plans include Japan, Germany, and Italy.

Garett says his best accomplishment was a presentation he gave to five hundred people, and his worst mistake was accidentally deleting some important computer data. What depresses him most is getting old, and his worst concern is not having enough time for the things he wants to do. He thinks that men are better off than women, because men approach things more logically, and that whites are better off than blacks in North America as well as elsewhere. He has no health concerns.

Garett detests no nation, but he likes Canada best. He does not want to become a celebrity, and his ambition is to build a family compound and open a restaurant. He aspires to lead a fulfilling life with no regrets, and his most cherished desire is to pass along his knowledge to the world. He believes that life's meaning consists of self-betterment and leaving things better than he found them.

Again, here we have a young man's concerns, interests, and outlook on life! His interests are somewhat different from his siblings, perhaps because he is the oldest and they had to depend on him a lot.

The Interests of Seniors

To compare the interests of juniors to the interests of seniors, I also interviewed four seniors.

For my first interview of a senior I chose my friend Pamela Sigvaldason. Pam is sixty, and lives in St. Albert, Alberta. Her ancestry is Scottish. She's a Chartered Accountant with a Bachelor of Mathematics degree, and is very intelligent and analytical. Pam is retired now, but performs volunteer work. She's a Christian and a member of the Anglican Church of Canada as well as the Girl Guides of Canada. She works diligently as a volunteer, and to regain her strength she sleeps an average of seven to eight hours.

Pam dislikes cooking and finds watching sports boring. She believes in the quality of life and to treat others as she would like to be treated – that's her philosophy. She loves both of her parents, hates no one, believes she has no enemies, and loves her husband, Eric, who is also her best friend, the most. Height scares her the most, and she finds snakes disgusting.

Pam's favorite pastime is reading, and her hobbies, besides reading, include knitting, sowing, and weaving. Her favorite sports are kayaking and skiing, and she also likes watching curling. Fruit salad is her favorite food, and she likes drinking coffee and wine. Her favorite movies are courtroom dramas and detective stories. She finds exploring nature exciting, and a play on words amusing. The most memorable events in her life were getting married and relocating. She likes travelling in Canada.

Pam says her best accomplishments were having and raising her children, and becoming a partner in Donnelly & Co. LLP. She says her worst mistake was getting engaged at age eighteen. What depresses her most is a feeling of lack of control, and her worst concern is her daughter's health. She thinks that men are better off than women [she gave no reason] and that, on the whole, perhaps whites are better off than blacks [again, no reason]. Her health concerns are maintaining healthy joints.

Pam detests nations that pick detestable leaders, and she likes Canada the most as a nation. She does not want to become a celebrity, and her ambition in life is giving back, to which she also aspires. She believes that life's meaning is looking up.

I have known Pam for over twenty years. She is a woman of the highest integrity with an extremely analytical mind. Her interests are somewhat more mature than those of the juniors I interviewed. Perhaps her additional education and experience have something to do with this. Thought-provoking, isn't it?

For my second interview of a senior I chose my friend Doug Gillis. Doug is seventy, and lives in Edmonton, Alberta. His ancestry is Scottish and English. He finished his second year university in commerce for accounting, and is best at planning. Doug is retired, but still performs volunteer work. He's a Christian Lutheran but not a member of a church or other group. He works diligently as a volunteer, and sleeps an average of nine hours to regain his strength.

Doug dislikes cleaning plumbing fixtures, and finds watching talk shows boring. He believes that someone is watching over us, and his philosophy is to give a stupid answer to a stupid question. Of his parents, he likes his father best. He loves his boys most, and hates most an obnoxious person he knows. He believes he has no enemies, and his wife, Wendy, is his best friend. Vaccinations scare him the most, and he finds professionals who misuse their patients disgusting.

Doug's favorite pastime is going for long walks, and his hobby is computer work. His favorite sport is golf, but he also likes watching football. Fish & chips is his favorite food, and beer is his favorite drink. His favorite movie is *Titanic*. He finds watching the Super

Bowl exciting and illogic amusing. The most memorable event in his life was his wedding day. Doug likes travelling to the towns of Banff and Jasper in Alberta.

He says his best accomplishment was setting up an electronic funds transfer system at a major insurance company, and his worst mistake was turning down good jobs for a so-called "safe" job. Canada's Prime Minister Justin Trudeau depresses him the most, and his biggest concern is becoming immobile – he has no other health concerns. He thinks that women are better off than men because they like to boss men, and that whites are better off than blacks, because blacks are more persecuted.

Doug detests Rwanda the most as a nation, and he likes the United States of America best as a nation. He does not want to become a celebrity, and his ambition in life is to keep going without help. Doug aspires to become a government advisory committee member, and his most cherished desire is to pay the least amount of tax possible. He believes that life's meaning is to pass on his wealth and knowledge to his children.

I have known Doug for about sixteen years. He is a very honest person and a good planner. His interests, naturally, are somewhat different than mine.

For my third interview of a senior I chose my

friend Patrick Barnes. Pat is seventy-one, and lives in Edmonton, Alberta. His ancestry is Irish and Scottish. He has a high-school education, and is best at working with people. Pat is retired, but is still teaching an estimating course and performs volunteer and trustee's work. He's a Christian and a member of the United Church, as well as a member of the Mill Woods Golf Club. He works diligently at the Edmonton People In Need Shelter Society's building program, and sleeps an average of six to eight hours to regain his strength.

Pat dislikes doing committee work, and unproductive committee work depresses him. He finds the soap opera *Coronation Street* boring. Pat believes that everybody has the right to decide for himself, and his philosophy is to accept people as they are. Of his parents, he likes his father best. He loves his wife, Delores, most, who is also his best friend. He believes he has no enemies and hates no one. Noisy machinery scares him the most, and he finds Donald Trump's politics disgusting.

Pat's favorite pastime is spending time with his family. His hobby as well as his favorite sport is golf, but he also likes watching hockey. Italian pasta is his favorite food, and red wine is his favorite drink. His favorite movie is *Dunkirk*. He finds travel in the Okanagan Valley exciting and Robin Williams amusing. The most memorable event in his life was a visit to an Aztec village. Pat likes travelling to the Shuswap in British Columbia, to Halifax in Nova Scotia, and to San Diego in California.

He says his best accomplishment was helping to develop a training center, and his worst mistake was picking a wrong business partner. His biggest concerns are the ailments of his friends, but he has no personal health concerns. He thinks that men are better off than women because they have more control of their destiny, and that whites are better off than blacks.

Pat does not detest any nation, but he likes Sweden the most. He does not want to become a celebrity, and his ambition in life is to stay healthy. His most cherished desire is to travel the world, and he believes that life's meaning is to leave more behind than one takes.

I have known Pat for many years. He is a very honest person and a good friend. He is definitely one of us ordinary folk!

For my last interview of a senior I chose my friend Frederick Soronow. My aim for this interview was that I wanted one more successful senior's interests for this chapter. Fred is sixty-eight, and lives in Richmond, BC. His ancestry is Jewish. He has a BA (Hons) university degree, and is best at finding solutions. Fred is a retired actuary. He is barely practicing the Jewish faith, does not believe in God or an afterlife, and is not a member of a religious institution or any other group. Fred's philosophy is to treat all people with kindness and respect. He sleeps six to seven hours to regain his strength.

Fred dislikes driving at night, and finds most comedies very infantile. Of his parents, he likes his father best. He loves his wife and sons most, and hates Donald Trump most. He does not have any enemies that he knows of, and his best friend is his first cousin. Falling and ending up crippled scares him the most, and he finds ethnic cleansing horrible and disgusting.

Fred's favorite pastime is watching TV, and his hobbies are following politics and watching his personal investments. His favorite sport is walking, but he also likes watching playoff hockey and basketball. Salmon is his favorite food, and coffee is his favorite drink. His favorite movie is *The Godfather*. Fred likes travelling to Hawaii. He finds spending time with his wife exciting and political talk shows interesting. The most memorable event in his life was the sudden death of a cherished lady friend.

He says his best accomplishment was raising kind and caring sons, and his worst mistake was spending too much time at the office. A very difficult life one of his sons is leading depresses him the most. His biggest concern is what may become of his son, and his other concern is his heart trouble. He thinks that men are better off than women, because men have it easier in life, and that whites are better off than blacks, because blacks are being discriminated against.

Fred says it's a tossup between Russia and the United States of America whom he detests the most as a nation, and he likes Canada the most as a nation. He does not want to become a celebrity, and his ambition in life is helping others. Fred aspires to be remembered as a good and decent man, and his most cherished desire is to live a long and healthy life, although he doesn't know if life has any meaning.

I have known Fred for about twenty-five years. He is a very thoughtful person and a good problem solver. His interests are not too different from mine, and he is also one of us ordinary folk!

The Wisdom of Ordinary Folk

Just before the end of 2017, I asked some of my friends and relatives the question, "What wisdom can you offer us for 2018?" Some of my friends and relatives ignored the question. Here are some of the answers I received:

- "Be kind to others, don't judge, and be the best version of yourself that you can be" are words of wisdom to live by in 2018.
- These are very unusual times. Pretty much anything can happen and with the US changing its view of the world and pulling back from international cooperation on many fronts these potential events are more likely to come to pass. All we can do is to keep calm, carry on, and try to be ready for the unexpected.
- My words of wisdom are: Try not to make the same mistakes that you made this year. Eat healthy, sleep well, exercise, have something to look forward to every day and wake up with a smile and a good morning kiss for your loved one every morning.

- For 2018...I think more equity appreciation in the short term; then, a serious correction.
- Hmm: I would say, live in the moment and take advantage of all these moments you get – you never know what might happen.
- 2018 should be a great year. All those years complaining about commuted values will finally bear fruit. The only problem I have is that I have to start drawing down my RRSPs, and I don't see any way around it.
- My operational philosophy is that "life is what you make it — your own two legs will take you where you want to go". Work hard and good things will ultimately happen.
- Be happy every day.
- Try to avoid it if you can.
- Wisdom for 2018: Investments: prudently fill alternatives mandates. Life: live your adventure.
- Be strong in your beliefs and kind to all people. I taught the kids if your life is like a garden and you plant peas, you will receive peas back.
- New Year's resolutions are temporary. A year-long goal is more fulfilling! My goal for 2018 is to make my health and happiness a priority.
- Fear hurts and love heals. All else is detail.
- My wisdom for 2018 is: Live each day to the fullest and just go with the flow!

- For 2018, I am offering the following words of wisdom, for myself! It is okay to sometimes feel sad, or to sometimes feel mad, and it is definitely okay to sometimes feel glad! Life can be a struggle, and sometimes it can be downright hard. I will allow myself to take a time-out when necessary, and I will understand when my loved ones need to do that too. I will try to remember that peace begins within me.

- I'm not so sure I have any wisdom to impart...I just read that due to Trump and North Korea, survival shelters are a growing industry. What a sad situation we have managed to put ourselves into. On the other hand, chocolate is also a growing industry as 9 out of 10 acknowledge a love for it. (The tenth is assumed to be lying.)

- Fiera as a firm remains optimistic about the Global economy and on stocks generally speaking. The Central banks should continue raising rates as the economies are growing at capacity. It could lead to higher commodity prices and for Canadian stocks to do better than in 2017.

- Love is something so precious; nobody should rush it unless they don't want it.

- My goal is to treat all with respect. Also my motto is "if you can dream it you can do it."

- Global economy looks good for 2018 and Canada might perform better than expected given the divide between the commodity movement and the stocks in the energy space.
- The wisdom of looking at something and checking it out – like having good judgement on buying stocks – instead of just buying for the sake of having. Listening and responding instead of reacting. That's how I'm going to start this year.
- Wherever you are, it is your family and friends who make your world. Give them the love and attention they deserve.
- Wisdom...Don't take life for granted and make the most of every day. Love, laugh, and find happiness. Make your happiness — don't look for it.
- Having a positive outlook is the only way to live! 2018 is the year of courage to make the changes that one has put off out of fear of the unknown! 2018 is the year to follow your dreams versus your fears! 2018 is the year to sort out one's personal affairs as they serve as the foundation for one's future. 2018 is the year where regrets have no place to reside!
- Write it on your heart that every day is the best day in the year. [Ralph Waldo Emerson]

- As for wisdom, I'd have to say "rise above the little things". Like always, it's important to pick your battles and what you put your energy towards.

- My thought: Surround yourself with positive influences, shun negativity, and stick to your values.

- Develop understanding and more patience. :)

- "Knowing when to impart it" is my response. I'm not being facetious; but given the general condition of our society, where everyone feels compelled to comment on everything (Facebook, Twitter, etc.), any wisdom that may exist is vastly diminished by the tremendous pool of collective ignorance. I define 'wisdom' as the practical application of intelligence (or experience), for the purpose of this response.

- My best insight is that we have to actively look after our physical, mental, and other health. It puts us in the best position to face whatever challenges come our way.

- My wisdom would be to enjoy what you have in the moment because you don't know when it could be gone.

- It is wise to perform acts of kindness either planned or random. It enhances physical and mental health.

- In terms of wisdom for 2018, take a break from everything that worries you every once in a while, and enjoy life's simple pleasures with your family.

Well, that's the wisdom I received from some of my friends and relatives – just ordinary folk. Isn't it interesting?

Identifying with Celebrities

Quite a number of us ordinary folk like to identify ourselves with celebrities, mostly actors, but also powerful leaders. In some respects, we're all actors, except that we do not follow a written script. Even some actors become ordinary folk in their private lives, when they do not follow a script.

One of my heroes was the actor Jimmy Stewart. I always felt that Jimmy was one of us ordinary folk, even in his movie roles. His movies I liked most are *Rear Window, Anatomy of a Murder, The Flight of the Phoenix,* and *Mr. Smith Goes to Washington.* Jimmy was born on May 20, 1908, and died on July 2, 1997, of pulmonary embolism. During World War II, he served as a US flier and led a bombing mission on December 13, 1943, on the German U-boat Facility at Kiel; on January 7, 1944, he was promoted to major, and ended up with a Distinguished Flying Cross award. On August 9, 1949, he married the model and actress Gloria Hatrick McLean, to whom he stayed married until her death on February 16, 1994. They had twin daughters born on May 7, 1951.

Jimmy's best friend was the actor Henry Fonda.

Henry's movie I like best is *12 Angry Men.* I think the movie has a very important message for us, namely how our prejudices affect our actions. I will come back to this movie in the chapter *All's Well that Ends Well.*

Other actors with whom I identified were Errol Flynn (when I was a boy), Joel McCrea, Gary Cooper, Gregory Peck, Robert Mitchum, Meryl Streep, and Nancy Olson. I liked Nancy Olson so much that my wife, Renate, and I decided to name our first daughter after her. Most of these actors led an admirable private life, which also impressed me besides their movie roles.

Some people like to identify with historical figures. A few years back, I had a business friend in Toronto who looked and acted a bit like Napoleon Bonaparte. My friend, too, was rather small – about five-foot-six – balding, and Italian. He liked using Napoleon Bonaparte's quotes in our business dealings. For example, we worked on a computer program together, and when I admired his ambition in the face of a few failures, he said, "Great ambition is the passion of a great character." I looked at him with some doubt, and he laughed. "Napoleon Bonaparte," he assured me. Two technicians were helping us with the project, and I thought they were rather unreasonable in their demands of my friend. When I mentioned this to him, he reminded me of another of Napoleon's quotes: "I would kiss a man's ass if I needed him." Well, what could I say to that? Then, when we were up against a problem which I considered impossible to resolve, he came back with: "Impossible is a word found only in a dictionary of fools." He laughed at my doubtful look and said, "Napoleon Bonaparte." In the end, we finished the project and it was a great success. My friend's beam perfectly imitated that of Napoleon Bonaparte's.

Many people identify with important politicians, especially if they like them. When I was a young man, I admired John Diefenbaker when he was the prime minister of Canada, and I followed most of his actions and speeches. Then, when he lost the election to Lester B. Pearson, I switched my attention to Pearson. However, when I listened to both their bickering in the House of Commons, I was soon disgusted with both of them, and I welcomed Pierre Elliot Trudeau when he took over as Prime Minister of Canada. He was younger than John Diefenbaker and Lester Pearson, and naturally appealed to younger Canadians. I had no trouble identifying with him. When John Diefenbaker was the Prime Minister of Canada, I also liked and identified with the American President John F. Kennedy, and I felt a great bereavement when he was assassinated.

In our contemporary world, it has become more difficult for some unknown reason to identify with world leaders, although I believe that many Americans identify with Donald Trump. His slogans like "Buy America, Hire American," and "Make America Great Again" are certainly appealing to many Americans. Some American people even love Donald Trump when he tells them, "I will build a great wall – and nobody builds walls better than me, believe me – and I'll build them very inexpensively. I will build a great, great wall on our southern border, and I will make Mexico pay for that wall. Mark my words."[*] Well, the future will tell, I guess.

Identifying with world leaders outside North America is more difficult because some of their issues are of less concern to us in North America. Take the issues German Chancellor Angela Merkel has been facing in the past year and especially in the past four months.[†] Her party, the Christian Democratic Union of Germany (CDU), has won the most seats in last September's election, but failed to win enough seats to form a majority government. In fact, it lost some seats because the people were unhappy with the party's refugee policy. Rather than submitting itself to new elections, the CDU decided to negotiate a coalition

---

[*] Quoted from the Piers Morgan interview.
[†] This chapter was written in February 2018.

with one or more other parties, and a coalition requires compromise.

Each party has its own platform of principles it wants to achieve, and it wants to maintain this platform if at all possible, but a total maintenance of a platform is not realistic when trying to reach an agreement with another party that wants to maintain a different platform. During the election campaign, each party runs down the platform of each other party, but during coalition negotiations, the parties must respect each other's platform to reach an agreement.

Of course, if a party wins a majority of seats it can almost completely ignore other parties' platforms, regardless of how beneficial these other platforms may be to the people. This is the opposite dilemma to the one the coalition poses. During elections, the people weigh the benefits or disadvantages of one platform against those of other platforms, and thus reach their decision for whom to vote. Some people may disregard the benefits of a party's platform if they are disappointed in the party's past performance. But when parties reach a coalition agreement, the people seldom get entirely what they hoped to attain when they voted.

These are the considerations required by anyone who wishes to identify with a world leader like Angela Merkel in her present quandary to form a coalition government. Angela Merkel has been a successful leader, and I wonder what more she is trying to achieve in the next four years, especially when having to fight with a hostile coalition party.

The British Prime Minister Theresa May has her problems as well. Having been saddled with a people's Brexit vote, she is trying to accomplish the best terms possible with the European Union, but she is also up against members of her own party who believe that the Brexit vote was a mistake and should be abandoned. Leaders like Theresa May seldom have a problem fighting legitimate opposition parties, but they get frustrated when having to cope with infighting. The reasons for leaving or remaining with the European Union are fairly evenly divided. Sure, Great Britain is separated from the rest of Europe by the English Channel, but it is still economically and politically part of Europe when it comes to defending Europe against its enemies. On the other hand, the British people desire to maintain their historical identity, which they are afraid they might lose when remaining in the European Union. This is the dilemma Theresa May is being asked to resolve.

The French President Emmanuel Macron has his problems too, but, I believe, he is well advised by his wife Brigitte Trogneux, who is twenty-four years older.

It seems to me that more and more women are asked to take over world leadership positions. Martin Schulz, the leader of the Social Democratic Party of Germany (SPD), who has been negotiating with Angela Merkel to form a coalition government, has announced he will step down as the party's leader and has nominated Andrea Nahles, leader of the Bundestag parliamentary group of the Social Democrats, and a former Federal Minister of Labor and Social Affairs and SPD Youth leader, to become his successor. However, another woman, the SPD mayor of the Northern German town of Flensburg, Simone Lange, has announced she will challenge Andrea Nahles for the SPD leadership. Thus, soon two women will lead the two largest parties in Germany. This women-leadership trend is apparent worldwide, with perhaps Russia as the exception.

The President of the Russian Federation, Vladimir Putin, did not yet have any women challengers for his presidency. He is another world leader I can readily identify with. Aside from some political mistakes, he does not lose his calm demeanor often, which is an important quality in a leader. Russian women seem to like him, and that is probably why they do not challenge his leadership.

Russia is actually part of Europe west of the Ural Mountain Range, and part of Asia east of the Ural

Mountain range. Will the European Russia ever become part of the European Union? I doubt it. But, as the saying goes, never is a long time! Who knows? If a woman will ever take over the leadership of Russia, I think it might be very possible that she will join the European Union. Of course, my opinion is prejudiced by the belief that women can achieve politically more than men. Men are too power-oriented.

What is Life's Meaning?

During the week of November 26, 2017, I asked some of my friends and relatives the question, "What, do you believe, is life's meaning?" The question taken literally could include plant and animal life, in which case the answers might have been "eat to live, and multiply." Note that I did not ask "What, do you believe, is your life's meaning?"

About half of my friends and relatives simply ignored the question, perhaps for lack of an answer, perhaps for being too busy to give me an answer. Some said life has no meaning, and most who decided to give me an answer related the question to them and gave me his or her life's personal meaning. Here are some of the answers I received:

- On reflection of mankind's history there is not ultimate purpose, or goal. Therefore, I believe each and every one of us is the answer. We each create and recreate our own meaning each time we interact with the world. As individuals we are free to make our own choices, but those choices shape the world around us and thus your meaning and the meaning of those around you keeps changing.

- Doing what's right and just for the betterment of the masses. I hope to do just that, Art. It's never been about just me.

- It seems to me that life is a series of lessons, joys, and obstacles, to prepare for the after-life. We never seem to be content or reach total happiness if only for short periods. But overall, we are part of a life cycle that seems to progress. Our life is part of the organism and we each have a role to play, programmed at birth. Hopefully we will find out who and why it was programmed in such a way in the afterlife.

- I believe that God created all things (speaking in general) and that we are here to worship and thank Him for what we are and have.

- One of the lines in Jesus' prayer was that God's kingdom of love would be on the earth as in heaven – or heaven on earth. God has given us a beautiful world and chosen to spread his love and life through his prized possession: man.
  Therefore, the meaning of life for me is: to be part of fulfilling this prayer, that because of my life, people will experience God's love – a little heaven on earth.

- Family.

- I believe that life's meaning is to be the person you are proud to be and to help those who seek the same to realize their goal and do so without regret! In short... live with purpose and pride!

- My quick answer would be: personal growth and enlightenment.

- I believe life's meaning is to find your purpose and discover your life's fullest potential.

- I think a person can drive himself crazy asking that question. "That way madness lies." I think the meaning of a person's life is quite possibly different for everybody.

- It is whatever each individual wants it to be. I just try to positively influence others.

- Hmm, tough question. I don't know. I think everyone has a purpose. The key is to find it. I have found that to be a difficult question as I tend to interrelate that to my set of values. One of my purposes is to help young disadvantaged people find a healthy life path through basketball.

- It's the pursuit and attainment of worthwhile goals, like: retire comfortably at age 65; assist my sons to establish themselves in good careers; and try to get an average of 5 strokes on every golf hole.

- From a spiritual perspective, one might suggest that the meaning of life is to make a journey of self-discovery in order to evolve to a higher form...From a non-spiritual perspective, one might suggest that we have been seeded on earth by an alien species, the sole purpose of which is to have us convert all available fuel sources to greenhouse gases, for reasons that we don't understand, but would presumably ultimately serve their purposes...I, for one, subscribe to the spiritual perspective, where we experience "life" as part of an overall process of evolvement.

- This is actually a pretty tough question for me right now. I'm dealing with a very ill parent. So I've thought about what life means for my mom and now me; leave things better than you found them and think big, try to have an impact and love bigger than you can imagine. How's that?

- The meaning or purpose of existence is: To control physical pleasures; to enhance psychological peace; and to utilize scientific methods developed by intelligent, educated people.

- For me life's meaning is about two things: reproduce and to create more good than bad in the world in every way (offspring, community, life, etc.).

- I am thinking seriously about this so would like a bit of time to respond. So, to me Life's meaning

38

or purpose is to give something back every day. To explain, I'm not referring to any major achievements to society. Instead I am referring to passing on kindnesses either by opening a door for someone, letting someone know I am thinking of them, making someone a meal when you know they are having difficulties, talking out a situation with a friend to help clarify meaning, mentoring a youth so that they can meet their dreams, providing positive feedback so that the message helps someone move forward in whatever their task is… small deeds.

- Hmm, probably to find something that makes you happy.

- I believe life is a journey, begin with a step, doing things that must be done along the way.

- My meaning is to walk with Jesus by my side or life would mean nothing to me – just overly fashionable – follow His commandments.

- If you were to ask the homeless man living on the street and then ask the man in the tailored suit rushing from the office tower, I would venture to say that the two answers would be entirely different. I have often ruminated over this question myself, for truly, what is life's meaning? A person might say, "Life is not fair" - and to a certain degree I would agree with that statement.

It is my belief that we are being questioned by life every single moment of every single day. Life's meaning to me is encompassed by my individual effort to consciously make choices that do not cause harm to others; to take a personal responsibility to seek out answers to life's problems, and to be the best that I can be, even in situations when life hasn't been fair!! I am grateful for my life, and that is very meaningful to me.

- Life's meaning to me is to be a good person and love and cherish life, health, and family. Leaving good memories of who you were and the people you help and touch in life.

- If I have to say it in few words, it will be the "existence of a human being."

- I try to figure that out every day. I don't know if anyone can know the meaning of life in their lifetime.

- The meaning of life to me is to be the best I can be and to lead by example. Help people who need help...but after rereading the question, I came up with a new answer: Do the things that keep you living and healthy. Reproduce to keep all life going — people, plants, and animals.

- You will never be happy if you continue to search for what happiness consists of. You will never live if you are looking for the meaning of life. Be the light that helps others see: it is what gives life its deepest significance. I believe life is precious, live every moment.

- For me, I do not really have any idea...too much confusion and stress. I can't think of a clear thought on the subject right now. Sorry.
- Life is...the effort you put in it.
- My experience suggests that the answer to this question changes over time. Therefore I won't know the answer until I finish living.

Well, there you have it. Some folks asked me: "What do you believe life's meaning is?" I gave them an answer similar to what I had written in my poems a few years back:

1971 was an eventful year for me. In business, competition was tough, and we were gearing up for computers to help us reduce our overhead. Personally, I lost my father. He came through a seemingly successful duodenum operation and later died of heart failure. I had not seen him for twenty-seven years – last, when he was on a short leave from his soldier duties during World War II.

I had planned on a trip to Germany for a reunion with him, and I felt bad for having it put off too long. Then, in December, just before Christmas, I was supervising the final connection of a high-voltage installation in a manhole, when undetected ground gas caused an explosion that blinded me for over two weeks. My mind was in turmoil, and my thoughts were challenging life's meaning. Suddenly, on Christmas Day, a seventy-two-line poem came into my mind, and I mean not created line by line, but it just appeared complete. Since I was blinded, I quickly called Renate, my wife, to bring pencil and paper, and I dictated the poem for her to write down. So often, when we get good ideas and do not write them down immediately, they disappear forever. This is how the poem *The Search for Life's Meaning* was born. The poem goes through various stages of search for life's meaning and culminates in the last six lines as follows:

Then, finally, you must give all back,
Which fell into your hands along the trek:
Your possessions, your mind, and even your heart,
To give human beings a better start.
This action will be your contribution
To the cycle of life and its evolution.

Everyday Cheats

We ordinary folk often complain about big cheaters, but how many of us are everyday cheaters, and what is the difference except the degree?

One day, I watched a family on a ferry from Tsawwassen to Swartz Bay. Father and mother were eating scrambled eggs, and their son was eating fresh oranges and grape fruit from three plastic bowls that were sold with lids on. He was picking away at all three bowls, and he finally finished one. The other two bowls were still nearly full, although he had poured some juice off of them. His father saw that the boy didn't want anymore and instructed him to put the lids back on the bowls and return them for a refund. The boy proceeded as instructed, but the cashier refused to take them back. I still wonder what would have happened to the two partially finished bowls if the cashier had have taken them back. This is just one example of everyday cheating.

Why is it that normally honest folk do not mind everyday cheats? This is most evident in road traffic: exceeding the speed limit; walking across an intersection on a red light; not coming to a complete stop at a stop sign; to mention a few. Even cities will employ questionable practices, like having a speed limit of 60 km/hr. along a stretch of the road and suddenly, for no apparent reason, changing the speed limit to 50 km/hr. to catch unaware drivers speeding. Some people also cheat themselves by defeating their diets or their New-Year's aim; some people think they're not lying when omitting part of the truth or by not being true to themselves; some people embellish an interview or a resume to make it seem that they know more than they do.

How many people ignore a missed item on a bill when they come to pay it? How many people do not declare all their income in a tax return? This could simply be small interest amounts on bank accounts, or some tips waiters or waitresses have received. However, how many rich folk thrive on unreported income? How many employees or managers claim fictitious expenses, or overcharge on an expense account? How many service suppliers overcharge for their services? How many employees claim more time on their time sheets than they have worked? How many employees exceed their allowed lunch or coffee breaks? How many people like jumping a queue to get ahead? And so on.

Some despicable cheating occurs when a service provider charges you for correcting his or her mistake;

or when a service provider wants cash to avoid sales tax; or when a service provider charges extra for the use of his or her tools that are already included in his or her charge-out rate; or when a service provider charges more based on what he or she thinks you can afford (this can also happen in a store that has no price tags on its products); or when service providers or manufacturers use cheaper quality materials and selling their products at a price of the more expensive quality materials; or when contractors renege on a valid undertaking; and so on.

One can also encounter incompetence with service providers. One time, I wanted a set of light pajamas for the hot summer months, and such pajamas were not available ready-made, so I bought some light, striped fabric, matching buttons, and elastic, and hired a seamstress recommended by the fabric store to sew them. I told the seamstress I wanted half-length sleeves. When I received the finished product, the sleeves were full-length, the pocket was made from different (white) fabric, the elastic was twisted, and the fly opening was on the left rather than the right side. I reported the mistakes to the seamstress and she said, no problem, for another $60.00 I can make the corrections. I decided to hire another seamstress to do so.

More serious cheating occurs when spouses

deceive each other; or when changing the price tag on a sales item in order to pay less for it; or claiming a refund on a well-used product; or falsifying a report card or any other document; or pocketing a product without paying for it; or adjusting the odometer before selling a car; or using a disabled sign without being disabled; or making something smaller and selling it for the same price as before; lots of food processors are doing this lately.

I have had an interesting experience with the latter. One time I ordered a Greek salad at a restaurant I frequented for lunch. It usually came with three slabs of feta cheese, but this time it only came with two slabs. I asked the waiter, why? He just shrugged his shoulders but reported my question to the manager. The manager came to my table and explained that the price of feta cheese had gone up, and he could no longer afford to supply three slabs for the price he charged for the salad. I said then why don't you increase the price for the salad? He said people might not want to pay a higher price for it. I told him, look, you also have a six-ounce steak on the menu. Would you just serve a five-ounce steak when the price of meat goes up? He got upset and said, if you don't like it, you can go and eat somewhere else. I took his advice. A few months later, I noticed a large closed sign at the restaurant.

Also, beware of airlines' flight-cancellation policies. Last October (2017), I had to cancel a flight to Bermuda with Air Canada, which I had booked on March 13, 2017. The airline told me that I had to use the credit (less the cancellation penalty, of course) before March 13, 2018. Then, in early February, 2018, I phoned the airline to book a flight to Montreal, Québec, in August that year, and the airline told me that this would cost me an additional penalty, because to get my full credit, less the cancellation penalty, I would have to fly to some destination prior to March 13, 2018. The airline customer service representative told me she was very sorry, but those were the airline's rules. As it happened, I had also intended to fly to Victoria, BC, but this flight would cost substantially less than the one I had booked to Bermuda. So, the airline customer service representative suggested that I book a business-class flight to use up as much as possible of the available credit. However, Air Canada does not have nonstop flights from Edmonton to Victoria – they stop in Vancouver – and business class is not available on the propeller-flight from Vancouver to Victoria. In any case, I had no other choice than to book this flight – at a substantial loss.

Another despicable cheat occurs through deceiving advertising. I assisted a retired relative with a dental problem recently. She wanted an irremovable prosthetic for her bottom teeth, as advertised by the dentist's brochure as follows: "You can choose a final prosthetic solution that is best for you, such as a fixed option (one with highest durability and chewing function, but cannot be removed) or a removable option (can be removed by you for easy cleaning)." The process required four implants, at a cost of $10,000, and a special prosthetic at a cost of $3,800. However, when the dental work was finished, she discovered that not only was the prosthetic removable, but it caused her quite a bit of pain, despite the promise of the same brochure, which reads: "…denture wearers often complain about problems and discomfort caused by their prosthesis…If you are experiencing similar problems…modern dental solutions can help you…" She eventually had to get help and a better solution from another dentist.

Buyers beware, as the saying goes! Many merchants and service providers have policies that border on cheating, and customers must protect themselves as much as possible not to be blindsided by them.

Acts of Treason

All nations have laws against treason. In some nations, treason is punished by death. Treason can have far reaching results. I have read that Adolf Hitler told one of his assistants, whom he trusted, that if Germany loses the war, it will be because of treason. Imagine: treason can even affect the outcome of a war.

The readers of my books know that I'm in the habit of pointing out strange things, and some of these strange things are language related. The word "treason" is one of these. Most people relate treason to betrayals of the state or the military. Few people think of treason as a betrayal of a person. Here is what the Merriam-Webster dictionary tells us:

1) The offense of attempting by overt acts to overthrow the government of the state to which the offender owes allegiance or to kill or personally injure the sovereign or the sovereign's family. 2) The betrayal of a trust. Merriam-Webster also offers the following example: "reading a friend's diary without permission would have to be regarded as the ultimate act of personal treason"

Clearly, Merriam-Webster in its treason definition "the betrayal of a trust" gives us an example of personal treason, which is a fairly remote use of the expression as far as most folks are concerned.

I have recently asked some of my friends and relatives the following question: "What example(s) can you give for what you believe are acts of treason, either in the arenas of politics, the military, business, marriage, or personal?" The key words in my question were "what you believe," therefore, what each person "believed" comprised an act of treason was what I was looking for. Here are some of the answers I received:

- I believe that treason is the act of giving secret information to an enemy. Defining who is an enemy is very arbitrary.
- Betrayal is treason so an example can be adultery or betraying ones trust.
- Technically, treason is betraying the country to which you are supposed to be loyal, so the term doesn't really apply to marriage, business, or personal relationships, although the term disloyal would apply in those situations. There are many acts of treason one could cite, but there are two sides to every story. I will give you two examples. When Claus von Stauffenburg and other conspirators attempted to assassinate Hitler,

was it an act of treason, or were they patriots to the German people? A recent example is that of Edward Snowden in releasing state secrets; treasonous or patriot?

- Treason can be narrowly defined as: sedition meaning disloyalty or treachery to one's country or its government. Treason is any attempt to overthrow the government or impair the well-being of a state to which one owes allegiance; the crime of giving aid or comfort to the enemies of one's government. But many expand its meaning to fit into their individual circumstances. On a personal level a treasonous act would include any act that completely violates shared trust, to the point that the trust can't be re-established. Examples could, but not always be: Infidelity in a marriage. A business partner purposely devaluing the partnership for the benefit of others. Or, it could be as simple as a close friend revealing closely held personal information with the intent to cause harm.

- Arnold Schwarzenegger having a kid out of wedlock with the maid and hiding it from his wife for years before she discovered it. This is marital treason. George Bush invading Iraq and telling Americans lies about weapon of mass destruction. That is treason to your country for being dishonest. I will personally always hold Jean Chrétien in high regards for standing up to the Americans and refusing to get involved as he knew better.

- Politics: wars of personal gain, greed, and fear. Business, marriage, and personal: betrayal of trust, i.e., extreme actions to hurt others for your own benefits.
- Omar Khadr, followed by Justin Trudeau, followed by Joshua Boyle, followed again by Justin Trudeau. My traditional definition of "treason" restricts it to betrayal of one's country, so I remain silent as to examples outside of that.
- Politics: overthrow political power for personal (singular) gain. And an example of that would be Hitler, while what is happening in Spain with Catalan I would call more democracy. Military: abandonment. Business: breaking your fiduciary duty. Marriage: leaving your partner without any warning. Personal: breaking a personal promise. Treason is the action of betraying someone or something, which everyone does every day without even knowing. You personally betray yourself when you don't keep your own promises. You betray your partner in marriage when you're not open about your feelings. You betray your business and associates when you do

not act ethically. You betray your officers and fellow comrades when you flee the military. And you betray your nation when you try to overthrow a government for a seemingly personal gain.

- In politics: if a person gives information from his country to another country. In business: it depends what business it is — not to give or sell trade secrets. In marriage: there are many as we well know; to forsake your partner is one.

- Treason is in the eye of the beholder. One person thinks you commit treason, the other person could see it a different way.

- I believe that treason in marriage is when a person's actions put their spouse in a vulnerable, undignified, or unsafe position. For example, if a husband publicly insults his wife to bring her shame, I see him as treasonous in his marriage.

- I believe any action that betrays a mutual commitment or agreement is treason. The complexity is that people tend to add a moral compass, political agenda, or humanitarian claim to that simple definition to broaden it and thereby justify many actions of treason that go unnamed as such.

- I think our mayor, premier, and prime minister all listen to their spouses too much when they make decisions.

- Personally, I believe that the ultimate treason, in a personal/marriage relationship sense, is when the person you trust and love the most stabs you in the back or becomes someone you barely know. For example, before I met X [her current boyfriend], I was in a two-year relationship with a family friend. We were really great from the start, but then I started noticing a few red flags here and there. Of course, I ignored them because I was so blinded by love. Over the time that we were together, I found out he had several other girls he kept in secret; still, I did not leave him, because he became very abusive — both physically and emotionally. I became scared and withdrawn, and I didn't want to tell anybody. It was like a trap! That's when I felt the most betrayed by someone.

- Cheating; putting others in danger.

- I would definitely say cheating in any form.

- An example of treason is Hillary Clinton and Benghazi. How she lied to protect herself. Bill and Monica Lewinsky: He also lied, then, later, confessed.

- Treason is ultimate disloyalty! We know there are many examples of treason in all facets of government, the military, business, and marriage. However, in choosing a specific example, I would say a father/mother would commit treason if he or she takes a significant amount of money that has been reserved for their child's education and gambles it in Las Vegas, losing it all. That to me would be treason. Just one example – there are unfortunately many.

- Maybe going behind someone's back without their approval.

- In the military, during the second World War, when the USA was developing the nuclear bomb an American working on the project leaked information to the Russians.

- I'd view treason as an act of deep betrayal, breaking of trust, usually related to a betrayal of a community/group/country. The only real acts of treason that come to mind are related to deceiving one's country by supporting a hostile counter-party with information or something of the sort. I wouldn't use the word treason for anything personal however, but that may be a personal preference.

- To me, treason is a strong word referring to extreme acts against someone or something and the person carrying out the act of treason is a traitor. Treason does not apply to the other issues in your first query; betrayal is possible in all cases but treason only relates to the state in my mind.

- Well, I can think of one recent example of treason in the Trump campaign team's collusion with Russia!

- Treason is always a betrayal of a trust; for example, when the world trusted the USA to honor the Paris accord and when Trump reneged on it that would be treason!

- When I hear the word treason I think of a person's betrayal to his/her government. It is also a matter of perspective for what is treason to one government may be loyalty to another. In a broader sense treason for me is a subset of the class of actions related to betrayal of a promise in the general sense...not just betrayal to country. Betrayal can occur to oneself, one's partner, business relationships, military, government, etc. For me, betrayal occurs when a person deliberately with knowledge and intent does not honor ones commitment or promise to another person or entity. In business, for me it comes down to meeting deadlines and providing actuarial services as expected by my clients. For my wife, it means supporting her for better or worse as we go through life. Trust in some ways is the opposite of betrayal. Trust is earned by honoring commitments as demonstrated by ones actions.

- In politics, Mulroney signing the Free Trade agreement after his head negotiator walked away saying it was a bad deal.

- I believe a very treasonous act was the release of all that secret information by that idiot Edward Snowden!

- The 1885 rebellion of Louis Riel in the province of Saskatchewan at the river landing of Batoche by the South Saskatchewan River. Louis led his Indian bands against the government troops to regain their land that was confiscated by the government. He surrendered and was taken to Regina for trial. He was condemned to hanging by Prime Minister John D. Macdonald.

- Whistleblowing is treason, yet altruistic. Any insider who alerts the public to illegal or unethical activities. Whistleblowing can be in any sphere, such as on Wall Street.

- Metaphorically speaking, one could ascertain that when one sells their soul to the devil even though they recognize that the price they must pay far surpasses their capacity to pay the price and then do it anyways because they have no choice – for example, payday loan firms!

- To me treason is a political term that is more used in the context of state or military. It is the gravest action of mistrust. In marriage, that would be cheating on your spouse. In business, it would be breaking confidentiality. In personal, it is losing someone's trust through actions such as lying or going behind someone's back.

Well, as you can see, the answers are varied but also similar. When using an expression like treason, one should be aware that people may assign different meanings to it.

Leaders Tainting Nations

When I think of the land where I was born, I think of it with mixed feelings. I think of Johann Wolfgang von Goethe, surely one of history's clearest thinkers; I think of Martin Luther, and his accomplishments translating the Bible into the German language – yet I'm puzzled by his antisemitism; I think of Frederick II, known as Frederick the Great, the only king of Germany called the Great; I think of Marlene Dietrich, the German actress who tried her luck in America; I think of Johann Sebastian Bach and Ludwig van Beethoven, the great German composers; I think of Curd Jürgens, another German actor who tried his luck in America; I think of Albert Einstein, the great physicist; I think of Johannes Gutenberg, who introduced printing to Europe with the printing press; I think of Otto von Bismarck, the Minister President of Prussia; I think of Pope Benedict XVI, who also suffered from the Nazi history; and so on.

I'm sure they were all great Germans. Naturally, I also think of Adolf Hitler, who came to Germany from Austria, and, within twelve years as German Chancellor, managed to make most people in the world forget about the historical greatness of Germany's people I mention above and focus their attention on the atrocities that took place during the twelve years of Hitler's reign.

I also think of Konrad Adenauer, who served as West German Chancellor from 1949 to 1963; I think of Helmut Kohl, who served as German Chancellor from 1982 to 1998 and focused on the process of integrating the former East Germany into the reunited Germany; I think of Willy Brandt, the West German Chancellor from 1969 to 1974, who tried to achieve reconciliation between West Germany and the countries of Eastern Europe; and I think of Angela Merkel, of course. All of these courageous German leaders tried, by their honorable actions, to obscure the ignominies of the Nazi period!

On the bright side, I think of Germany now: her industry, her economy, her place in the European Union, her leadership, like Angela Merkel, and I wonder if her historical greatness can again be achieved. Certainly, the will to do so is there. Certainly, people with the ability are there. And, hopefully, the encouragement of other nations will be there!

A country can be as beautiful as a multicolored field of tulips, but its people will not be judged by its beauty but by the reputation of its leaders. The

German people, just ordinary folk like ordinary folk everywhere, are still judged, to some extent, by the reputation of Adolf Hitler, whom they allowed to assume power over them!

At present,[*] the American people are judged by the questionable actions of their President Donald Trump, whom they elected; the British people are judged by the strengths and weaknesses of their Prime Minister Theresa May, whom they elected; the French people are judged by the determination of their President Emmanuel Macron, whom they recently elected; the German people are presently waiting for a coalition government to be formed; until last fall, they were judged by their Chancellor Angela Merkel's performance; the world admired her as a strong leader, except for her determination to allow a million refugees into the country, which was seen by the world and the German people as a mistake; this mistake cost her party, the Christian Democratic Union (CDU), sixty-five seats in the September 2017 elections.[†]

Each party has a platform, on which it seeks elections, and during coalition negotiations some principles of their platform must be sacrificed by the

---

[*] January 2018

[†] The Christian Democratic Union is down from 311 to 246 seats, although the Social Democrats also lost forty seats: down from 193 to 153 – 355 seats are required for a majority in the Bundestag.

parties, and other principles must be accepted. Furthermore, the leadership of the country must be agreed upon. The world is quite familiar with Angela Merkel's leadership but not too familiar with Martin Schulz. Martin Schulz is a year younger than Angela Merkel. He previously was President of the European Parliament from 2012 to 2017, Leader of the Progressive Alliance of Socialists and Democrats from 2004 to 2012, and a Member of the European Parliament from Germany from 1994 to 2017. In November 2016, Schulz announced he would not seek a third term as President of the European Parliament, but instead would stand in 2017 as the SPD candidate to become Chancellor of Germany. So, Martin Schulz is also experienced enough for Germany's leadership.

However, regardless of the outcome of coalition negotiations on platform principles, Angela Merkel will probably continue as Germany's Chancellor.

All's Well that Ends Well

This proverb is widely in use. Many children learn it from childhood days. My wise mother instilled it to me before I started school: Ende gut, alles gut – all's well that ends well! Much later, I asked myself: does a good outcome always justify poor means to get there? I decided it doesn't. However, it would not surprise me if the parents of Adolf Hitler, Joseph Stalin, Benito Mussolini, and Francisco Franco instilled the same idea to them. Hitler's belief that all's well that ends well also led him to the attitude that winning is the only thing that counts. He passed this attitude on to some of his immediate followers when he told them that a victor does not have to account for his deeds to get there, and he applied this philosophy also to his lies, when he said: The victor will never be asked if he told the truth.

All through history, people who started wars believed in this proverb! This belief cost an estimated 85 million soldiers and civilians their lives during World War II. To get them to fight a war in the first place, German soldiers had embossed in their belt buckles the words: GOTT MIT UNS – God with us.

So, they were led to believe that, when God is with them, how can their fights not end well? The American General George S. Patton told his soldiers: The object of war is not to die for your country but to make the other bastard die for his. And the "other bastard," of course, was the German soldier, who had been given a similar command by his officers.

My father was sent to the swamps in Finland by the German army. He told me that it was so swampy that he couldn't sleep on the ground, so he buckled his belt, which was extra-long, around a small tree trunk and his chest, and hung there during the night trying to catch some sleep. Only his lower legs were in the swamp, and soon they became diseased. He was still alive when World War II ended, while an estimated 5.3 million of his comrades had died for their country! All's well that ends well, for him, except for the disease in his lower legs, and the loss of his home, his wife, and his children.

Joseph Stalin, too, took George Patton's command to heart when he caused many million Russians to die for their country, simply because he suspected them of treason.

Some of you may be familiar with my book *Critical Reflections,* which has a chapter called *Prejudicial Movies.* Well, many movies have also been made with the proverb in mind: all's well that ends well. The protagonist can do almost anything, as long as all ends well. *Judge John Deed* is a British legal drama television series produced by the BBC, and in one of its episodes a prisoner kills another prisoner, who was a never successfully convicted pedophile. The accused murderer claimed a defense of preventing future child abuses, and the jury found him innocent, even though his killing action was recorded by a surveillance camera. This is a movie that takes the proverb all's well that ends well to an extreme.

In another movie, the adverse of this proverb is not so obvious. The movie is called *12 Angry Men.* My comments are in connection to a 1957 American courtroom drama film, where twelve men on a jury have to decide the guilt or innocence of a boy accused of killing his father. An initial vote is taken in the jury room, and eleven men voted guilty while one of them, Juror #8 (Henry Fonda), voted not guilty. An angry discussion ensues to convince Juror #8 to change his mind, but Juror #8 stands firm. After a while of nonproductive discussions, Juror #8 proposes that the other eleven jurors take a secret ballot to determine if some jurors have changed their minds. He said if all still voted guilty, he would not stand in the way of a conviction, but if one or more side with him, they would continue their discussions.

This proposal by Juror #8 was a mistake, I

believe, and the script should have been changed. Juror #8 had a reasonable doubt regarding the boy's guilt, and eventual discussions among the jurors proved him right. So, had all eleven jurors voted guilty, Juror #8 would have been responsible for sending an innocent boy to his death. As it turned out in the script, Juror #9 sided with Juror #8, and the resulting discussions finally found the boy not guilty. Nevertheless, even though a script can cause "all's well that ends well" to happen, in real life Juror #8's proposal could easily have backfired! To avoid this kind of criticism, Henry Fonda (Juror #8) who was also a producer of the film, should have insisted on a script change that would still have brought out the biases and prejudices and personal conflicts that were involved and brought to light by the film.

There are literally thousands of examples where us ordinary folk have been brainwashed into believing that all's well that ends well, when this belief in many cases endorses bad, or even criminal, behavior because of an accidental or wanted good outcome.

Creation vs. Evolution

Most of us ordinary folk believe that God has created the human being, despite Charles Darwin's theory of evolution. Even scientists who believe in Darwin's evolution theory must admit that there is something attractive about the creation theory.

Examining a human being, with a vertebra to keep him erect, with arms and legs to enable him to work and walk, with lungs to let him breathe, with eyes to let him see, with a nose to let him smell, with a mouth to let him taste and eat his food, with a stomach to digest his food, with bowels to process and eliminate his digested food, with kidneys to process his liquid intake, with a bladder and tubes to store and shed his processed liquid intake, with a brain and a mind to reason out complex problems, and so on, you wonder how such a marvelous creation could have evolved from a microscopic living being in a mire with the essential ingredients for life billions of years ago. But evolutionists will tell you that the human being has evolved from such a microscopic being, hard as it may be to believe by a creationist.

Does it matter whether we were created or

evolved? I think it does! The simple general purpose
of evolution is to eat to stay alive and to multiply to
save the species. However, creation usually has a more
specific purpose. So, if we evolved, the purpose is
simple, but if we were created, the question is, for
what purpose? Henceforth, I shall engage in some
speculations to answer this question – just to satisfy
creationists, since I, too, believe in evolution.

I could use Buddhism or some other Eastern
religion and reincarnation as a starting point, but I
prefer the Bible, because most of us ordinary folk are
familiar with the Bible – at least in the West. Now,
there are some peculiar aspects that must be taken into
account when it comes to the creation theory of the
Bible. The first aspect is the existence of God; the
second aspect is that God, the Creator, was not alone
in His creation of man; and the third aspect is that God
allowed his "sons" to come to Earth and marry the
daughters of human beings.

If we can agree that God should be the Supreme
Existence in our Universe, we should also agree that
the Biblical God does not meet this criterion – He is
too emotional for a Supreme Existence! In my view,
the Supreme Existence in our Universe consists of our
universal laws that govern everything in our Universe,
and that Supreme Existence is God. Therefore,
naturally, God must exist!

The second aspect, that God, the (Biblical) Creator, was not alone in His creation of man is based on the Biblical assertion "God said, let us make man in our image, after our likeness" (note the plural) – Genesis 1:26. The third aspect can be found in Genesis 6:2: "the sons of God saw the daughter of men that they were fair; and they took them wives of all which they chose."

All three aspects easily lead us to conclude that the Biblical God and his cohorts and sons were aliens, which is also supported in other parts of the Bible, like The Acts 14:11: "The gods are come down to us in the likeness of men."[*] However, this does not answer the question: For what purpose did they create man on Earth? Let me give you a reasonable explanation as an answer: Suppose highly advanced aliens needed to find a new abode; they searched the Universe and found Earth, and on Earth they found an underdeveloped species resembling them. Then, they went to work to upgrade this species. Why? They did this to save their own alien species, of course. Thus, every aspect makes sense, even the aspect of God's sons coming to Earth to marry human women. In fact, my proposition satisfies not only the creational aspect but also the evolutional aspect.

---

[*] Erich von Däniken gives us more examples in his book *Chariots of the Gods*. Also, see my book *Conclusions Volume I.*

Aliens' visit to Earth to upgrade human beings also makes sense when you consider that billions of years of evolution have only produced a backward species. Religious folk might not like my proposition, but if they are also Bible adherents, they must admit that this sacred book suggests this proposition. Other religions, like Scientology, admit alien visits as well.

Here is an interesting quote from UK's Daily Express: "RELIGIONS on Earth were created by aliens who visited Earth thousands of years ago, it has shockingly been claimed....A new conspiracy theory says, before religious texts like the Bible were written, alien lifeforms visited Earth and were seen as "gods" by the more primitive humans."

Visiting aliens who educated and improved the human race would certainly explain the rapid development of human beings in the last ten thousand years, after billions of years crawling out of mud puddles, followed by the tedious and elaborate evolution that eventually led to Homo erectus.

God Willing

I have already devoted a chapter on fatalism in my book *Human Traits & follies*. However, as I frequently encountered the trait among us ordinary folk, I decided to devote another chapter on the subject in this book.

"God willing" is one of those meaningless expressions that many people use without thought. Using the term thoughtlessly is one thing, but using the term intentionally is another matter. In the latter case, the person using the term could be a fatalist, and the term could represent a cop-out. People will say: we're planning to take a trip to Hawaii this year, God willing. Then, if they do not take the trip, God was not willing to let them take it. If they believe this nonsense, they are called fatalists. Fatalism is the doctrine that events are fixed in advance; therefore, human beings are powerless to change them.

Fatalists can blame anything they want on God. Anything that happens is because God was willing for it to happen, and anything that does not happen is because God was not willing for it to happen. This is a very convenient way to live one's life. One literally does not have to do anything because God looks after everything. It is a convenient cop-out for doing nothing. To a fatalist, since everything is preordained, he or she can never take responsibility for his or her actions – it's all God's doing! When people tell me "God willing" my first response is, "Do you really mean this?" And if they tell me "yes," I know I'm dealing with a fatalist. The American Journal of Health Behavior tells us that a person with fatalistic beliefs perceives health as being beyond one's control and instead dependent on chance, luck, fate, or God.

One can never win an occurrence argument with a fatalist. If a fatalist says that our climate is caused by the universal laws designed by God, and one tells the fatalist that perhaps our scientists will find ways to influence our climate, the fatalist will simply assert that this can only happen if God wills it to happen. To a fatalist, everything our scientists create is preordained.

My father had a duodenum operation at age 61; the operation was successful, but soon afterwards he died of heart failure. This happened in May 1971. For over ten years, I had already promised myself to visit him in Northern Germany, and I felt bad that I failed to do so before he died. I reread the letters he sent me in the 1950s, and I was surprised how many times he mentioned "God willing." He was not even upset with me for failing to visit him, because this would have also upset him with God. He was a genuine fatalist. Had he not been drafted by the German army in February 1942, he may have influenced me to become a fatalist as well. After that time, I only saw him a few more times during his leaves.

One type of fatalism is the so-called *Idle Argument.* Origen and Cicero described it thus [Wikipedia]:

- If it is fated for you to recover from this illness, then you will recover whether you call a doctor or not.
- Likewise, if you are fated not to recover, you will not do so whether you call a doctor or not.
- But either it is fated that you will recover from this illness, or it is fated that you will not recover.
- Therefore, it is futile to consult a doctor.

However, this argument fails to consider that those fated to recover may also be those fated to consult a doctor.

To end this chapter with a little humor, I have asked the authors of the book *Plato and a Platypus Walk into a Bar...*, Thomas Cathcart and Daniel Klein, for permission to reprint the following five paragraphs:

…there are some determinists who say, "God made me do it. In fact, God has determined everything in the universe down to the last detail." Baruch Spinoza, the seventeenth-century Dutch/Jewish philosopher, and Jonathan Edwards, the eighteenth-century American theologian, were proponents of this sort of theological determinism. The eagle, the frog, and the truck driver in the following story all probably thought they chose and executed their actions freely.

Moses, Jesus, and a bearded old man are playing golf. Moses drives a long one, which lands on the fairway but rolls directly towards the pond. Moses raises his club, parts the water, and the ball rolls safely to the other side.

Jesus also hits a long one towards the same pond, but just as it's about to land in the center, it hovers above the surface. Jesus casually walks out on the pond and chips it onto the green.

The bearded man's drive hits a fence and bounces out onto the street, where it caroms off an oncoming truck and back onto the fairway. It's headed directly for the pond, but it lands on a lily pad, where a frog sees it and snatches it into his mouth. An eagle swoops down, grabs the frog, and flies away. As the eagle and the frog pass over the green, the frog drops the ball, and it lands in the cup for a hole-in-one.

Moses turns to Jesus and says, "I hate playing with your dad."

The End is Near

The November 14, 2016, *Time* magazine front cover page had a picture of Donald Trump and Hillary Clinton holding a white sign with the words "THE END IS NEAR" on it. They were probably referring to their campaigns, but it reminded me of the multitude of predictions we hear about our world coming to an end. Many doomsday predictors, ancient and modern, have told us when to expect the end of our world. It has never happened and probably never will happen. But if an intelligence agency reported that it had discovered evidence of an irresponsible nation planning to destroy the world with nuclear weapons, perhaps we should pay attention.

The picture of Donald Trump and Hillary Clinton with their sign also reminded me of Paul the Apostle's words, in his second letter to Timothy: "…in the last days perilous times shall come. For men shall be lovers of their own selves, covetous, boasters, proud, blasphemers, disobedient to parents, unthankful, unholy, without natural affection, trucebreakers, false accusers, incontinent, fierce, despisers of those that are good, traitors, heady, highminded, lovers of pleasures more than lovers of God; having a form of godliness, but denying the power thereof…" (II. Timothy 3:1-5) I hope you fully appreciate the Apostle Paul's nonsensical end-of-world predictions, because these happenings had already occurred repeatedly for thousands of years prior to his times.

Nostradamus, a French apothecary (1503-1566), was another apocalypse predictor. However, many sceptics were unconvinced by Nostradamus's premonitions. Brian Dunning, science writer and creator of the Skeptoid Podcast, asserted that Nostradamus's quatrains had been misinterpreted and mistranslated over the years and should be ignored. Nostradamus's critics all agree that the vast majority of his predictions have failed to pass and those that did require a strong dose of hindsight and imagination to connect them even remotely to historical events.

Prior to the twentieth century, there were at least a hundred doomsday predictions. The Jewish Essene sect of ascetics predicted one between the years 66 and 70 AD. The French bishop Martin of Tours predicted the world would end before 400 AD. The Christian historian Sextus Julius Africanus predicted the year 800 AD. Pope Sylvester II was sure the end of the world would occur in the year 1000 AD. Various Christians were certain it would be 1033 AD, a thousand years after the death of Jesus. Pope Innocent

III was sure it would be 1284 AD, 666 years after the rise of Islam. Martin Luther predicted the end of the world no later than 1600 AD. Christopher Columbus predicted either 1656 or 1658 AD. The mathematician Jacob Bernoutti predicted a comet would destroy Earth on April 15, 1719 AD. The Catholic Apostolic Church, founded in 1831 AD, predicted the end of the world after the last one of its founders died, which happened in 1901 AD.

Then, after 1901, the International Bible Students Association predicted the spring of 1918. Margaret Rowan, the Seventh-day Adventist, claimed that the angel Gabriel appeared before her and told her the world would end at midnight on February 13, 1925. The Jehovah's Witnesses, a group that branched off from the Bible Student movement, predicted the end in 1941. John Ballou Newbrough, the author of *OASPE: A New Bible*, predicted 1947. Jim Jones, the founder of the People's Temple, predicted a nuclear holocaust for 1967. Marshall Applewhite, the leader of the Heaven's Gate cult, claimed a spacecraft was trailing Comet Hale-Bopp and that suicide was the only way to evacuate Earth so that their souls could board the spacecraft; thus, he and thirty-eight of his followers committed mass suicide in 1997. Isaac Newton, Edgar Cayce, Ed Dobson, and Lester Sumrall all predicted the end of the world in the year 2000.

The Hermetic Order of the Golden Dawn predicted the year 2010. Predictions for upcoming years include the prophecy of the Messiah Foundation International for the year 2026. The Talmud of Orthodox Judaism predicts 2239 for the end of the world.

Our scientists also offer predictions for the end of Earth. Most of these predictions involve natural disasters, like asteroids hitting Earth, and are thousands and millions of years into the future, but even if none of these disasters should occur, most scientists are in agreement that the universal heat death will eventually do us in, but this heat death is ten duotrigintillion years in the future.

Most of us refuse to pay any more attention to end-of-world predictions. However, I want you to give some thought to a February 2018 news article, which I copied: "A new species of all-female crayfish able to reproduce without males is multiplying rapidly and invading ecosystems across the world." Let us just think about the implications for a minute. Since female crayfish can reproduce without males, what about humans? If human females find a way to reproduce without the help of us males, will this be the end of the world for us males? Think about it. Females may tell us, "Enough is enough of male abuse; now it's our turn."

Appendix: The Millionaires' Club

I have had another dream: this one about a millionaires' club. The club had no members but only patrons who were willing to make donations. The specified donations consisted of $100,000, $500,000, or $1,000,000. The club owned a building for the purpose of donation administration and disbursements, and to cook and serve steaks to patrons.

When a patron entered the building, he or she would stop at a table in the lobby and pick up a glass with a lit candle in it. A small glass would be for a $100,000 donation, a medium-sized glass for a $500,000 donation, and a larger glass for a $1,000,000 donation. The patron would then proceed to the dining room.

In the dining room, the patron would pick a table and place the glass on the table. A server would come and take the steak order. The steaks offered were New York strips, filet mignons, rib eyes, and T-bone, with a baked potato. Patrons could also request a salad with their choice of dressing, and French bread with pads of butter. Bottled Fiji water was served without ice, but patrons could request ice produced from Fiji water. A light beer (3% alcohol) especially brewed for the club was available upon request, but wine or stronger spirits were not available. Various steak sauces were also available upon request.

All steaks were of high-quality beef, and were fried over charcoal on an open hearth in the dining room, and when served to the patron the server would remove the glass with the candle, request a signed chit for the donation, and issue a receipt for tax purposes.

The mission of the club was to keep the human race alive as much as possible. The Club would use the donations to send CARE Packages anywhere in the world where famine persevered.

Acknowledgements

I wish to thank my grandchildren who agreed to share their lives' interests and activities with us, and who responded to some of my questions, namely, *Jordan, Samantha, Megan,* and *Garett.* I also wish to thank my friends *Pam Sigvaldason, Doug Gillis, Pat Barnes,* and *Fred Soronow*, for sharing their interests and activities with us.

Next, I wish to thank those friends and relatives who responded to my questions regarding their offers of wisdom for 2018, and/or their beliefs regarding life's meaning, and/or their examples regarding acts of treason, namely, *Ron Abraham, Tammy Anast, Natalie Antonio, Bailey Archer, Jim Bendfeld, Susan Bird, Pei San Chan, Brandon Ellement, Dennis Ellement, Birgit Gates, Doug Gillis, Ida Doreida Gjormarkaj, Rob Hatchwell, David Hoffmann, Vickie Hon, Donald Jenion, Bernie Jeske, Wally Kusters, Jim Lampard, Carol Letcher, Ed Lee, Kevin Levy, Diana Llorente, Bob Lynn, Lilliana Martino, Barbara Melnyk, Kelly Morris, Bill Munro, Farrell O'Malley, Tim Osztovits, Tara Petersen, Mario Richard, Daniella Rickards, Andrea Schmelcher, Pam Sigvaldason, Nicole Smit,*

Fred Soronow, Karin Thormann, John White, Philip Wierciszewski, Shannon Williams, and *Wayne Wilson.*

In addition, I wish to thank my daughters *Nancy* and *Diana* for contributing a few ideas regarding everyday cheats, as well as to thank them for helping me proofread the manuscript. All mistakes remaining are entirely mine.

I should also mention that for some references I made use of the *Wikipedia*, to whom I donate occasionally.

Last but not least, I wish to thank *Daniel Klein* and *Thomas Cathcart* for allowing me to use an excerpt from their book *Plato and a Platypus Walk into a Bar...*

Without *Wikipedia* references, and the input of these people, the book would not be what it is.

About the Author

Arthur O.R. Thormann was born 1934 in Berlin,
Germany, and emigrated to Canada in 1951.
Canadians are among the freest thinkers of the world
and a great people, and Arthur decided to join them as
a fellow citizen. Edmonton, Alberta, is his hometown.

www.ingramcontent.com/pod-product-compliance
Lightning Source LLC
Chambersburg PA
CBHW071827020426
42331CB00007B/1638